Mullá Ḥusayn

The Story of the Declaration of the Báb for Young Children

Written by Alhan Rahimi

Illustrations by Alina Onipchenko

Copyright © 2019, 2021 by Alhan Rahimi
alhan@persianarabic.com

ISBN: 978-1-990286-00-1 (Hardcover)
ISBN: 978-1-096919-70-4 (Paperback)

Written by Alhan Rahimi based on true historical events

Illustrations by Alina Onipchenko

Cover design by Alina Onipchenko &
Anahit Aleksanyan

All rights reserved worldwide. No part of this book may be reproduced, distributed or transmitted in any form or by any means without the prior written permission of the author, except in the case of brief quotations embodied in critical reviews.

This book has been approved by the National Spiritual Assembly of the Bahá'ís of Canada.

Once upon a time...

...There was a young man named Mullá Ḥusayn. He lived in a country called Persia.

Mullá Ḥusayn had a teacher he loved very much. His teacher's name was Siyyid Kázim.

Siyyid Kázim taught many things to his students. He told them about a Treasure they had to find. The Treasure was a special person sent by God. He was called The Promised One because it was a promise that God would send Him.

Siyyid Kázim asked his students to leave their homes and go to different places to search for the promised One.

Mullá Ḥusayn immediately listened to his teacher. First, he went to a place of prayer called mosque, and stayed there for forty days. He prayed and prayed and prayed. He asked God to help him find the promised One.

He felt in his heart that something was pulling him to a city called S̲híráz, so he travelled there with two of his friends.

When they arrived at the gate of S̲híráz, he asked his friends to go to the mosque and wait for him there.

As he was outside the gate, suddenly he saw a young Person approaching him and welcoming him with a smile. He was wearing a green turban on His head. He invited Mullá Ḥusayn to His home to refresh himself after the long journey.

Mullá Ḥusayn was impressed by this Person and felt that something was different about Him. He accepted His invitation.

They arrived at the gate of a house. "Enter therein in peace, secure," said the young Host. Mullá Ḥusayn had special feelings in his heart. He wondered if this visit would help him find the promised One he was looking for.

They went upstairs and sat in a beautiful room. His Host ordered for a water jug to be brought, and He Himself poured water over the hands of Mullá Ḥusayn to wash away the dust of the journey.

Then He offered Mullá Ḥusayn a refreshing drink. After that, He personally prepared tea for Mullá Ḥusayn, using the samovar, and offered it to him.

After sunset, the Host started talking to Mullá Ḥusayn about important things. He asked him about his teacher, Siyyid Kázim. Mullá Ḥusayn told Him that Siyyid Kázim asked his students to go to different places, and to find the promised One that was sent by God and follow Him.

His Host wondered if Siyyid Kázim told his students any special details about the promised One that Mullá Ḥusayn was looking for. Mullá Ḥusayn told Him that his teacher gave them some signs about the promised One. He said all the signs. One of them was His innate knowledge. That meant the promised One would know everything without anyone teaching it to Him and without going to school.

Mullá Ḥusayn's Host paused and then said in a vibrant voice, "Behold, all these signs are manifest in Me!"

He mentioned each of the signs that Mullá Ḥusayn had told him, and showed him that they were all true about Him.

Mullá Ḥusayn was very surprised. Could this Person really be the promised One he was looking for?

Mullá Ḥusayn had always wanted his teacher to write something about a holy text called the Súrih of Joseph. However, his teacher did not do this, telling Mullá Ḥusayn that the promised One would write it for him instead.

Suddenly, without Mullá Ḥusayn saying a single word, his Host said to him, "Now is the time to reveal the commentary on the Súrih of Joseph."

This was the moment Mullá Ḥusayn knew that this Person was the One he had been searching for. He had finally found the promised One.

This promised One was called The Báb, which means The Gate in the Arabic language. He was the Gate to God.

That same night, the Báb told Mullá Ḥusayn, "This night, this very hour will, in the days to come, be celebrated as one of the greatest and most significant of all festivals."

This special visit was on the evening of May 22nd, 1844.

How do you celebrate this day? Do you have any pictures to glue to this page? You can also draw something about this celebration if you like.

If you were wondering about all the signs that Siyyid Kázim told his students about the promised One, here they are:

1. He is of a pure lineage.
2. He is one of the descendants of Fáṭimih (the daughter of Prophet Muḥammad).
3. His age is more than twenty and less than thirty.
4. He has innate knowledge.
5. His height is medium.
6. He does not smoke.
7. His physical body is healthy.

A prayer revealed by the Báb

Say: God sufficeth all things above all things, and nothing in the heavens or in the earth but God sufficeth. Verily, He is in Himself the Knower, the Sustainer, the Omnipotent.

Acknowledgements

- My husband Varqa for his continuous support
- The National Spiritual Assembly of the Bahá'ís of Canada for their approval of this book in a timely manner
- My illustrator, Alina Onipchenko, for her patience with my numerous requests of changes and for bringing the story to life
- My friend and illustrator of a previous book, Anahit Aleksanyan, for helping with the design of the cover
- My friends Noora Rowhani, Maha Halabecki & Tracy Holman for their opinions and suggestions

A note to the friends of Bahá'ís who read this book...

If it's your first time hearing about this story and you'd like to know a more detailed version of it, you may visit this webpage

https://www.bahai.org/the-bab/life-the-bab

However, you can read the full story in the books mentioned in the "References" section.

References:

The Dawn-Breakers: Nabíl's Narrative of the Early Days of the Bahá'í Revelation

Ruhi Book 4